7/07

Famous Places of the World

Australia

Helen Bateman and Jayne Denshire

Smart Apple Media

Smart Apple Media
2140 Howard Drive West
North Mankato
Minnesota 56003

First published in 2006 by
MACMILLAN EDUCATION AUSTRALIA PTY LTD
627 Chapel Street, South Yarra, Australia 3141

Visit our Web site at www.macmillan.com.au

Associated companies and representatives throughout the world.

Library of Congress Cataloging-in-Publication Data

Bateman, Helen.
    Australia / by Helen Bateman and Jayne Denshire.
      p. cm. — (Famous places of the world)
    Includes index.
    ISBN-13: 978-1-58340-798-1 (alk. paper)
    1. Australia—Juvenile literature. 2. Australia—Geography—Juvenile literature.
    I. Denshire, Jayne. II. Title.

    DU96B37 2006
    994—dc22   2006002521

Project management by Limelight Press Pty Ltd
Design by Stan Lamond, Lamond Art & Design
Illustrations by Marjorie Crosby-Fairall
Maps by Lamond Art & Design and Andrew Davies
Map icons by Andrew Davies
Research by Kathy Gerrard
Consultant: Colin Sale BA (Sydney) MSc (London)

Printed in the United States

Acknowledgments
The authors and the publisher are grateful to the following for permission to reproduce copyright material:

Cover photograph: Ulura with desert vegetation, courtesy of Lonely Planet/John Banagan
APL/Corbis/Theo Allofs p. 10; Federation Square Images/ Peter Hyatt p. 23 (bottom); Getty Images/ Gavriel Jecan p. 15; Getty Images/John Banagan p. 16; Getty Images/ Christopher Groenhout p. 28; iStockphoto/Edward Hor p. 4 (centre left); iStockphoto/Pieter Schockaert p. 4 (centre right); iStockphoto/Nicholas Rjabow p. 18; Stan Lamond p. 8; Lonely Planet/Michael Aw p. 11; Lonely Planet/ John Banagan p. 22; Lonely Planet/John Banagan p. 23 (top); Lonely Planet/Christopher Groenhout p. 24; Lonely Planet/John Banagan p. 25 (top); Lonely Planet/John Banagan p. 27; Lonely Planet/ Manfred Gottschalk p. 29; Robert Armstrong/Photolibrary.com p. 6; Phillip Hayson/Photolibrary.com p. 7; Robert Francis/Photolibrary.com p. 9; Stefan Mokrzecki/Photolibrary p. 12; David Messent/ Photolibrary.com p. 13; Halaska Jacob/Photolibrary.com p. 17; George Hall/Photolibrary.com p. 19 (top); Topham Picturepoint/Photolibrary p. 19 (bottom); Richard Ashworth/Photolibrary.com p. 21; Jocelyn Burt/Photolibrary.com p. 25; Brian Lovell/Photolibrary.com p. 26; Reuters/Parks Victoria/handout/Picture Media p. 17 (top).

While every care has been taken to trace and acknowledge copyright, the publisher tenders their apologies for any accidental infringement where copyright has proved untraceable. Where the attempt has been unsuccessful, the publisher welcomes information that would redress the situation.

Contents

When a word in the text is printed in **bold**. You can look up its meaning in the Glossary on page 31.

Wonders of Australia

Australia is a **continent** of extremes, from lush tropical **habitats** to dry deserts. Tiny outback towns, coastal beaches, and big cities all give Australia a unique character. There are many famous places in Australia, some ancient and some modern. Some are natural wonders and some have been built by humans.

What makes a place famous?

The most common reasons why places become famous are because of their:

- **formation** how they were formed by nature
- **construction** how they were built by humans
- **antiquity** their age, dating back to ancient times
- **size** their height, width, length, volume, or area
- **function** how they work, or what they are used for
- **cultural importance** their value to the customs and society of the country
- **religious importance** their value to the religious beliefs of the country

ZOOM IN
Australia is the only country in the world to occupy a whole continent.

Famous places in Australia

Australia has many famous places. Some are built structures and some are features created by nature.

Key

- Sydney Opera House
- Parliament House
- Sydney Harbour Bridge
- Coober Pedy
- Kakadu National Park
- Uluru-Kata Tjuta National Park
- Sydney Harbour Bridge
- Port Arthur
- Great Barrier Reef
- Twelve Apostles
- Federation Square
- Pinnacles Desert
- Bungle Bungle Range

Sydney Opera House

FACT FINDER

Location **Sydney Harbour, New South Wales**

Date built **1959–1973**

Height **tallest shell is 197 feet (60 m)**

Sydney Opera House is a built structure that is famous for its cultural importance and construction. It is Australia's most famous performing arts venue and is known throughout the world for its distinctive design.

A prize-winner

A competition was held to find the best design for the Sydney Opera House. Danish architect Joern Utzon won. His design features three groups of shell structures that lock together and sit above a massive granite slab. The design fits perfectly with the harbour location and creates an effect of movement on water, a bit like sails or wings. The building includes four performance halls, rehearsal space, and restaurants.

ZOOM IN
The idea for the curved shape of the sail structures came from orange segments, not from white sails.

◄ The shells of the roof are covered with over a million ceramic tiles. They look like fish scales when the light catches them.

A long process

Construction took more than 10 years and in that time many problems arose. The building was erected in three stages. The podium, or base, was built first, then the shell roofs, and finally the inside areas. The shells are supported by fan-shaped concrete beams and thick concrete walls. Glass walls fill the open ends of the shells, allowing spectacular views from virtually every area. A walkway encircles the entire building and links to each performance space.

This world-famous building is a masterpiece and is being considered for the World Heritage list.

▲ Sydney Opera House sits on Bennelong Point, in the heart of Sydney Harbour.

ZOOM IN
The glass walls that fill the ends and sides of the shells look like falling water.

Kakadu National Park

ZOOM IN
About one-third of all Australia's birds are found in Kakadu National Park.

FACT FINDER

Location east of Darwin, Northern Territory

Size 7,700 square miles (20,000 sq km)

National Park since 1979

WORLD HERITAGE SITE since 1981 (extended in 1987 and 1992)

Kakadu National Park is a natural feature that is famous for its beauty and cultural importance. Rolling hills, rocky outcrops, rain forests, **wetlands**, waterfalls, and rivers are all a part of this ever-changing landscape. The park is also rich in Indigenous Australian history and culture. The wet and dry seasons encourage unique plant and animal life. Much of this wildlife is native to this **ecosystem**.

▼ Kakadu's unique ecosystem includes wetlands and provides a habitat for a wide range of rare plants and animals.

Traditional owners

Indigenous Australians have occupied the region for 50,000 years. Local rock art tells about Indigenous life and spiritual connections with the land. The traditional owners and the Commonwealth Department of Environment and Heritage jointly manage the park. The land is owned by the indigenous groups who live there and they lease it to the Commonwealth.

Rich in wildlife

Kakadu's **flora** is among the most beautiful in Australia, with over 1,700 known plant varieties. Much of Kakadu is covered with open eucalypt forest, however plants that survive with and without water for long periods also thrive. About 60 **species** of **mammal** live in the park, including **marsupials** such as kangaroos and quolls. The most famous reptile there is the crocodile. This unique national park is known around the world for its beauty and cultural heritage.

▲ These rock paintings tell stories about Indigenous Australian creation and culture. They were found at a sacred rock shelter in Kakadu called Nourlangie Rock.

INSIDE STORY

Uranium and other minerals lie under the ground in many parts of Kakadu National Park. Some companies want to set up mines in the National Park and drill for these valuable minerals, but many people feel mining will destroy the area's natural beauty. One of the biggest mines in the area is Jabiluka. The Mirarr people, who are the traditional owners of the land where Jabiluka is, have set up the Gundjehmi Aboriginal Corporation to help protect Kakadu from unnecessary mining.

ZOOM IN
Kakadu National Park is one of only 22 World Heritage Sites listed for both their natural and cultural value.

Great Barrier Reef

The Great Barrier Reef is a natural feature that is famous for its formation, size, and beauty. It is the longest coral reef in the world. A very large number of plant and animal species live in this rich wildlife habitat, considered to be one of the world's greatest natural wonders.

Indigenous Australians have hunted turtles in these waters for hundreds of years.

ZOOM IN

Captain Cook discovered the Great Barrier Reef in 1770 while he was mapping the waters of Australia's east coast.

▼ The Great Barrier Reef runs along the northeast coast of Queensland. It has 2,900 separate reefs and over 300 coral and sand islands called cays.

Coral under the surface

The Great Barrier Reef is made of coral, which lies under or just above the surface of the ocean. The coral has a hard **limestone** shell with living creatures called polyps, inside it. Polyps continually die then grow again. Most of the reef is made up of the empty skeletons of dead polyps.

A wide world of fish

Large numbers of brightly colored fish fill the waters surrounding the reef, including clown fish and the dangerous scorpion fish. Humpback whales also breed in the area.

Many things threaten the survival of living coral on the Great Barrier Reef. Tropical hurricanes, overfishing and the poisonous effects of the crown-of-thorns starfish can all shorten the life of coral. However, the greatest recent threat is **global warming**. If the reef waters stay too warm for too long, the coral loses its life-giving color and dies.

This beautiful natural wonder is now **protected** so that it will be **preserved** for the future.

▲ The waters of the Great Barrier Reef are home to 1,500 different kinds of fish and many beautiful coral formations.

ZOOM IN
Astronauts can see the Great Barrier Reef from the Moon.

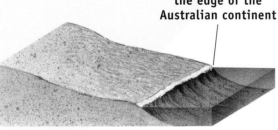

coral grows along the edge of the Australian continent

1. Coral first grew along the coastal edge of the Australian continent.

coral reef is now a barrier offshore after sea level rises

2. As the sea level rose, the coral reef grew and formed a barrier off the shoreline.

Parliament House

Parliament House is a built structure that is famous for its construction and cultural importance. This example of modern architecture sits at the top of Capital Hill against a backdrop of gardens and parklands. Parliament House is actually a number of buildings, set out in different sections. The buildings are the place of Australian government and are some of Australia's most notable buildings.

ZOOM IN
A large tapestry of Arthur Boyd's painting of the Australian bush hangs in the Great Hall.

Room after room

There are over 4,000 rooms in Parliament House. The main foyer, which has a marble finish, leads into the dining area called the Great Hall. This space opens onto the Members Hall. Areas for the Senate and the House of Representatives are either side of this. Parliament House is built entirely of Australian materials including a variety of timbers and stones.

A flagpole sits between the House of Representatives and Senate rooms. It has four stainless steel legs, each one 266 feet (81 m) high, that support the flag. The flagpole is one of the world's largest stainless steel structures.

◄ A giant mosaic designed by Michael Tjakamarra covers the forecourt of Parliament House. It is called "Meeting Place" and represents a gathering of tribes.

Extending Canberra's plan

The design for Parliament House was an extension of the original plan for Canberra, created by Walter Burley Griffin in 1911.

Today it stands as a symbol of Australian government.

forecourt

flagpole

Members Hall

Senate

House of Representatives

Ministerial wing

▲ When viewed from above, the Senate and House of Representatives buildings form the shape of two arcs with the flagpole between.

Uluru–Kata Tjuta National Park

FACT FINDER

Location southwest of Alice Springs, Northern Territory

Size 488 square miles (1,325 sq km)

National Park since the 1940s

WORLD HERITAGE SITE since 1987

Uluru–Kata Tjuta National Park is a natural feature that is famous for its formation and cultural importance. It is where two unusual rock formations are found called Uluru, one rock, and Kata Tjuta, a collection of rocks. The park is close to the centre of Australia in the traditional lands of the Pitjantjatjara and Yankunytjatjara people.

ZOOM IN

The traditional owners prefer visitors not to climb Uluru as a mark of respect for Indigenous law and culture.

▼ Uluru is 1,132 feet (345 m) high, 1.5 miles (2.4 km) long and 1 mile (1.6 km) wide. It takes two hours to walk around the base, a distance of 5.6 miles (9 km).

▲ Kata Tjuta stretches for 13.5 square miles (35 sq km) and comprises 36 huge rounded sandstone rock formations. The highest one is 1,138 feet (347 m).

Uluru, the "great pebble"

Uluru is one of the largest **monoliths** in the world. It is made from pebbly sandstone that contains a mineral called feldspar. The feldspar in the rock changes color, depending on where the sun is, and glows a vivid red color at sunrise and sunset. The vegetation around Uluru is mainly low and scrubby. Desert oaks, spinifex grass, and thousands of wild flowers cover the flat surrounding area.

Kata Tjuta's "many heads"

Kata Tjuta is a Pitjantjatjara word meaning "many heads." Many of the formations in this rock group have carvings that tell stories about traditional life in the area. However, Kata Tjuta is a sacred place in Anangu men's law and many of their stories cannot be publicly told. The **heritage** of Uluru–Kata Tjuta National Park makes it a unique cultural area.

ZOOM IN

"Tjukurpa" is the traditional law of Anangu, which guides them in their daily lives.

INSIDE STORY

In 1985, the governor-general of Australia handed ownership of Uluru and Kata Tjuta back to Anangu, the local Indigenous Australians. For many years, this area had not been well looked after by non-Indigenous Australians and many of the traditional Indigenous laws had been ignored. Now the Uluru–Kata Tjuta National Park is jointly managed by the Uluru–Kata Tjuta Board of Management and Parks Australia. The traditional laws of the land are used to better care for this sacred area.

Twelve Apostles

FACT FINDER

Location **Great Ocean Road, Victoria**

Date formed **over the last 20 million years**

Height **up to 148 feet (45 m)**

The Twelve Apostles are natural landforms that are famous for their formation. These strange rock stacks jut out of the waters of the treacherous Southern Ocean along a stretch of coast at Port Campbell. Now only eight formations remain, but it is not clear how many there were originally.

► The Twelve Apostles sit beside limestone cliffs. The cliffs have been eroded over millions of years by blasting winds and crashing seas.

this stack collapsed and is now a pile of rubble

ZOOM IN
This stretch of coastline is known as the "Shipwreck Coast" because over 140 ships have been destroyed and hundreds of lives lost there.

Giant formations

These giant sandstone formations have formed over millions of years. They are actually very small islands that have been shaped as the limestone cliffs near them were **eroded** by severe winds and big seas. At one stage, these formations were attached to a rocky shoreline.

Whalers and sealers

Whalers and **sealers** were the first white people to live along this section of coast in the early 1800s. They came in ships, in search of a new place to settle. Many of their ships were wrecked in the wild seas.

Two of the major rock formations have collapsed in recent years. One fell down in 2005 and the other, known as London Bridge, collapsed about ten years before.

These natural wonders are best known for their unusual formation.

▼ Over time, some of the stacks have collapsed. Recently, one fell down without warning into a pile of rubble.

collapsed rock

ZOOM IN
The Twelve Apostles were originally called the Sow and Piglets. A nearby island represented the sow and the rock formations, the piglets.

▶ Sunrise and sunset are the best times to view the rock formations. At these times of day, their shapes form silhouettes against the blazing tones of light.

Sydney Harbour Bridge

FACT FINDER

Location Sydney Harbour, New South Wales

Date opened 1932

Width 160.1 feet (48.8 m)

Height of arch 440 feet (134 m) above water level

Length 0.7 miles (1.15 km)

Weight 52,000 tons (52,800 tonnes)

Sydney Harbour Bridge is a built structure that is famous for its construction. It is the world's largest steel **arch bridge**. The bridge links Sydney's centre with the North Shore. Prior to it being built, people mainly caught ferries to and from the North Shore. Traffic on the bridge has increased a lot since it was built. In 1932 the average number of vehicles per day was 11,000. Now it is around 160,000 vehicles.

▼ Arch bridges are one of the oldest types of bridge and are very strong. The bridge's weight is carried along the curve to the supports at each end.

Concrete and steel

Sydney Harbour Bridge is built of concrete and steel. Two pairs of concrete and granite **pylons** sit at each end of the steel arch and support the structure. The bridge carries eight lanes of road traffic and has two railway tracks, a cycle path and a footpath.

Bridge building

Construction of Sydney Harbour Bridge began in 1924 and took 1,400 men eight years to complete. The bridge was built in stages. First the **reinforced concrete** foundations were laid. Next, the **abutments** and **approach spans** were built. Then the main arch was formed, and finally the steel decking was hung from the arch. This massive bridge is known for its distinctive shape and harbour setting.

▼ In 1929 construction on the arch began with a half-arch being built from each shore. The arch was successfully joined in 1930.

▲ People are able to do a bridge climb to the top of the arch. They can see a view of Sydney Harbour in all directions.

ZOOM IN
This bridge is affectionately known as "The Coat hanger" because of its arched shape. The top of the arch rises and falls about 7 inches (18 cm) due to changes in the temperature.

Bungle Bungle Range

The Bungle Bungle Range is a natural landform that is famous for its formation, beauty and cultural importance. Unusual rock formations with distinctive markings stretch for hundreds of kilometers in this area, which is part of the Purnululu National Park. The Kija people live in this region. These Indigenous Australians have been making use of plant and animal life there for many years.

ZOOM IN
The name "Bungle Bungle" is thought to come from the name for the area in the local Kija language.

▼ The beehive-shaped domes have been formed from the processes of rock weathering and erosion within the cracks over a long time.

Striking stripy domes

Rock domes shaped like beehives and formed from ancient sandstone are found throughout the Bungle Bungle Range. The domes are striped with bands of orange and black. The black stripes are black **algae** that grows through the moist layers of the rocks, and the orange stripes are where mineral stains have built up on the surface. The range also features magnificent **gorges** and caves, high cliffs, and clear pools.

A rare find

Many unique plant species are found in the Bungle Bungles. A rare palm species called *Livistonia* grows in many of the gorges and waterholes and is native to the area. The baobab, also called the boab or bottle tree, is an unusual tree with a strange, swollen trunk and tangled branches.

History, culture, and nature combine to make this landmark a unique famous place.

▲ Cathedral Gorge is in the Bungle Bungles. If you make a noise in the space created between the steep, rocky walls, the sound will echo loudly.

INSIDE STORY

Although Indigenous Australians have lived in the Bungle Bungles for thousands of years, there has only recently been a road into the region. The creative thinking of a local Kimberley man helped find a ground route into the area. He flew a spotter plane low over the area, throwing sacks of flour out of the aircraft as he went, to mark the easiest route into the Bungles. A four-wheel drive vehicle later followed the dusty flour trail and found an easy way in by road.

ZOOM IN
Twice as many people see the range from the air as visit it by road.

Federation Square

Federation Square is a series of built structures that are famous for their construction and cultural importance. The modern architecture seen in the square is positioned in Melbourne's historic centre. It fills an entire city block and is a community meeting place for social and cultural activities.

On deck

Federation Square sits on a huge deck that has been built over Melbourne's original railway yards. Its design allows for many uses. Various buildings including the atrium, galleries, restaurants, and offices link together via a series of diagonal routes. The central plaza is stepped to allow for the rising levels of the railway tracks below.

▼ Federation Square has a number of buildings around a plaza. The paving in the plaza is made from Kimberley sandstone.

Time and people

Federation Square took six years to build and needed more than 5,000 people to complete the project. During that time there were many disagreements over the design, budget, and timing for the project.

The outside of some of the square's main buildings are covered with **three-dimensional** triangles made from zinc, glass and sandstone.

This is one of Australia's newest famous places that is fast developing a reputation for its clever construction and cultural importance.

ZOOM IN
The decking for the square contains springs, which lessen the effect of vibrations on the buildings and noise from the trains.

ZOOM IN
Over 22,000 triangular tiles make up the outside surfaces of Federation Square.

▶ The effect created by the triangular shapes on the outside of the buildings is like an abstract sculpture.

◀ The atrium is a covered open space and is made from glass and steel.

Coober Pedy

Coober Pedy is a built habitat that is famous for its construction and function. The town produces over 80 percent of the world's **opals**. Many of its buildings are built underground because of the intense heat in summer and the cold nights in winter. Living and working underground is a way of life in Coober Pedy.

ZOOM IN

The "Olympic Australis" is reported to be the largest and most valuable gem opal ever found at Coober Pedy. It was named after the Olympic Games held in Melbourne in 1956, the same year the opal was found.

▼ Coober Pedy is one of Australia's most isolated towns, hundreds of miles from the nearest settlement.

24

Underground jewel

Opal mining is Coober Pedy's main industry. Common and precious opals are found. The beautiful colors in the precious gem come from the unusual **silica** mineral crystals. Opal mines at Coober Pedy are between 16 and 98 feet (5–30 m) under the ground. To look for opals, a **shaft** is sunk down by machine then a tunnel is dug along the **seam** of rock.

Cool living

To survive the heat, miners build **dugouts** to live in under the ground where the temperature is always the same. Many of these are converted mines.

Living and working under the ground make Coober Pedy a unique outback town.

▼ Many different dwellings are built underground, from homes and shops to churches and restaurants.

INSIDE STORY

The first opal discovered in Coober Pedy was by a 14-year-old boy named Willie Hutchinson. Willie was left to look after the camp while his gold-prospecting friends went in search of water. While they were away, he decided to look for water himself in the nearby range. After a while, he returned to camp carrying half a sugar sack full of opals, and a huge smile on his face.

opal

▲ Only 5 percent of opals found at Coober Pedy are precious. The rest, like this one, are common opals.

Port Arthur

Port Arthur is a built structure that is famous for its function and cultural importance. It was first built as a timber station but quickly became a convict settlement during the 1800s. Port Arthur is known for its harsh treatment of the convicts who were held in its **penitentiary**. Many of the convicts had committed serious crimes in New South Wales.

ZOOM IN
Fifteen large ships and over 140 smaller vessels, from whaleboats to rowboats, were built by the prisoners.

▼ Port Arthur sits on a strip of land surrounded by water. At the narrow end of the site, called Eaglehawk Neck, guard dogs stopped prisoners escaping.

► A separate prison block was built at Port Arthur in 1848. Prisoners were sent to cells there that had no light and were soundproof, as punishment for their crimes.

Prisoners at work

The prisoners at Port Arthur were made to work hard on different building projects, such as a huge flour mill and a hospital. They were treated harshly by the guards and were **flogged** if they disobeyed orders. The settlement grew into an industrial centre for shipbuilding, shoe making, timber and brick making.

Life after prison

The **penal settlement** closed in 1877 and soon after, the place was renamed Carnarvon and a township began to grow. Eventually the town had its own post office and sporting clubs. In the early 1900s Carnarvon was renamed Port Arthur again and it became a popular place to visit for its historic value.

In 1996, many people were shot at Port Arthur by a gunman. This event became known worldwide and led to tougher gun laws in Australia.

INSIDE STORY

The prisoners at Port Arthur often tried to escape. One man, Billy Hunt, draped a kangaroo skin over his back and tried to flee from the grounds. The guards, who were not fed well, saw what they thought was a tasty meal in the distance and tried to shoot. Scared he would get shot, Hunt threw off his disguise and gave himself up.

ZOOM IN
One out of every seven prisoners died at Port Arthur. They are buried on the nearby Island of the Dead.

The Pinnacles Desert

Location Nambung National Park, Western Australia

Date discovered by white settlers 1849

Area 0.7 square miles (2 sq km)

Highest pillar 11.5 feet (3.5 m)

The Pinnacles Desert is a natural area that is famous for its formation. Thousands of huge limestone pillars, or pinnacles, rise up from the shifting yellow sands of this desert. The pinnacles have formed over thousands of years and have been shaped by the effects of wind and rain.

▼ While most animals in this desert are night-dwellers, it is not uncommon to see an emu dart across the desert sands in the daytime.

FORMATION OF PINNACLES

DURING FORMATION

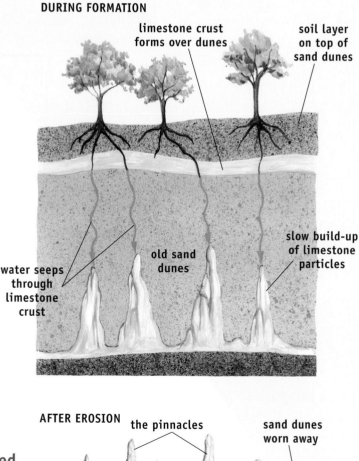

limestone crust forms over dunes

soil layer on top of sand dunes

water seeps through limestone crust

old sand dunes

slow build-up of limestone particles

AFTER EROSION

the pinnacles

sand dunes worn away

► The pinnacles first formed under the ground. They appeared above the ground once the moving desert sands had been worn away.

28

From sea to desert

The limestone material of the pinnacles was originally shells from sea creatures that existed in the area in an earlier period of history. The shells were broken into sand and brought ashore by waves. The sand was then carried inland by wind to form high, moving sand dunes. It is thought that the pinnacles have been covered by moving sands then uncovered by wind more than once throughout history.

Alive with color

From August to October each year, the area around the Pinnacles Desert bursts into color. A vast array of wildflowers bloom and create a spectacular sight.

The pinnacle shapes that appear in this desert are a most unusual sight. Their remarkable formation makes them one of Australia's most famous natural wonders.

▲ Some pillars are tall and pointy, others are more rounded. They can be as small as a mouse or as high as a bus.

ZOOM IN
Each pinnacle probably extends deep into the ground. Only its tip shows above the ground, much like an iceberg.

Famous places of Australia

Our world has a rich collection of famous places. Some are spectacular natural wonders and some are engineering or architectural masterpieces. These famous places in Australia are outstanding in many different ways.

Wonders formed by nature

PLACE	FAMOUS FOR
Kakadu National Park	Its unique ecosystem of rare plants and animals Its Indigenous Australian history and culture
Great Barrier Reef	Longest coral reef in the world Largest structure in the world made by living things
Uluru–Kata Tjuta National Park	Unusual large rock formations in Central Australia Its Indigenous Australian history and culture
Twelve Apostles	Unusual rock formations on the coast
Bungle Bungle Range	Eroded rock domes with layers of different colors
Pinnacles Desert	Huge limestone pillars rising out of the desert

Masterpieces built by humans

PLACE	FAMOUS FOR
Sydney Opera House	Its distinctive modern architecture and harbour location
Parliament House	Home of Australian government Its architecture and design
Sydney Harbour Bridge	Largest steel arch bridge in the world Its harbour location
Federation Square	Its modern architecture and design
Coober Pedy	Produces over 80 percent of the world's opals Underground dwellings
Port Arthur	Convict settlement in the 1800s Shooting massacre in 1996

Glossary

abutments structures that support the ends of a bridge at the shore

algae water plants with no stems or leaves

approach spans parts of a steel arch bridge that lead to the main arch

arch bridge a curved structure, resting on supports at each end that take the bridge's weight

continent one of the main land masses of the world

dugouts underground dwellings

ecosystem a community of living things living in balance with each other

eroded cracked and worn away by the elements of weather, such as water, wind, and ice

flogged beaten hard with a whip or stick

flora the plants of a particular area

global warming the rise in temperature of the whole of the Earth's atmosphere or air

gorges narrow valleys with steep, rocky walls on both sides of a river or stream

habitats places where plants or animals naturally grow

heritage the culture and traditions of a place

limestone a soft, white, chalk-like rock

mammal an animal whose young feeds on its mother's milk

marsupials mammals that keep and feed their young in a pouch after their birth until they can look after themselves

monoliths single huge rocks or stones

opals valuable gems of various colors

penal settlement a place for punishment of criminals

penitentiary prison

preserved kept safe

protected guarded from injury or danger

pylons the two tall structures either end of an arch bridge

reinforced concrete concrete that is strengthened with steel bars

sealers people who hunt seals

seam a thin layer of a different type of rock or mineral in the ground

shaft an enclosed space that leads down into the ground

silica a substance with crystals that is found in some minerals and rocks

species a group of animals or plants that can reproduce their own kind

three-dimensional having height, width, and depth

whalers people who hunt whales

wetlands an area where the soil is often wet or underwater, such as a swamp or marsh

Index